KT-432-904

Kitchen favourites

Kitchen favourites

The small print

EGGS We use medium eggs, unless otherwise stated. Pregnant women, the elderly and children should avoid recipes with eggs which are raw or not fully cooked.

FRUIT AND VEGETABLES Recipes use medium-size fruit and veg, unless otherwise stated.

LIGHT SOFT CHEESE Where a recipe uses reduced-fat soft cheese, we mean a soft cheese with 30% less fat than its full-fat equivalent.

LOW-FAT SPREAD When a recipe uses a low-fat spread, we mean a spread with a fat content of no more than 39%.

MICROWAVES If we have used a microwave in any of our recipes, the timings will be for an 850-watt microwave oven.

PREP AND COOK TIMES These are approximate and meant to be guidelines only. The prep time includes all the steps up to and following the main cooking time(s). The stated cook times may vary according to your oven.

VEGETARIAN HARD ITALIAN CHEESE Where we reference this in vegetarian recipes, we mean a cheese similar to Parmesan (which is not vegetarian) but which is suitable for vegetarians.

GLUTEN FREE Recipes displaying the gluten free icon include ingredients that naturally do not contain gluten, but may also contain processed products, such as sauces, stock cubes and spice mixes. If so, you should ensure that those products do not include any gluten-containing ingredients (wheat, barley or rye) – these will be highlighted in the ingredients list on the product's label. Manufacturers may also indicate whether there is a chance that their product may have been accidentally contaminated with gluten during the manufacturing process. For more information and guidance on gluten-free products, visit www.coeliac.org.uk

SMARTPOINTS have been calculated using the values for generic foods, not brands (except where stated). Tracking using branded items may affect the recorded SmartPoints.

WHEN YOU SEE THESE SYMBOLS:

 Tells you how many SmartPoints are in the recipe.

 Indicates a recipe is suitable for freezing.

 Indicates a No Count recipe.

 Indicates a recipe is gluten free or can be made gluten free with a few simple swaps, for example by using gluten free soy sauce.

V Indicates a recipe is vegetarian.

Seven.

Produced by Seven Publishing on behalf of Weight Watchers International, Inc. Published February 2017. All rights reserved. No part of this publication may be reproduced, stored in a retrieval system or transmitted in any form by any means, electronic, mechanical photocopying, recording or otherwise, without the prior written permission of Seven Publishing.

First published in Great Britain by Seven Publishing Ltd. Copyright © 2017, Weight Watchers International, Inc.

Seven Publishing Ltd
3-7 Herbal Hill
London
EC1R 5EJ
www.seven.co.uk

This book is copyright under the Berne Convention. No reproduction without permission. All rights reserved.

10 9 8 7 6 5 4 3 2 1

Weight Watchers SmartPoints and the SmartPoints icon are the registered trademarks of Weight Watchers International, Inc and are used under licence by Weight Watchers (UK) Ltd. All rights reserved.

A CIP catalogue record for this book is available from the British Library.
ISBN: 978-0-9935835-5-1

WEIGHT WATCHERS PUBLICATIONS TEAM
Imogen Prescott, Samantha Rees, Nicola Kirk, Steph Williams, Ruby Bamford.

FOR SEVEN PUBLISHING LTD
FOOD
Food editor Sarah Akhurst
Food assistants Linzi Brechin, Nadine Brown, Gabriella English

EDITORIAL
Editor in Chief Helen Renshaw
Editor Ward Hellewell **Sub editors** Sarah Allen, Chloe Hay

DESIGN & PHOTOGRAPHY
Art director Liz Baird
Main shoot team: Photographer Ria Osborne
Food stylists Sarah Cook, Ellie Jarvis
Prop stylist Tonia Shuttleworth
Other photographs: Terry Benson, Tony Briscoe, Mike English, Scott Grummett, Jonathan Kennedy, Bill Kingston, Kris Kirkham, Lauren Mclean, David Munns, Noel Murphy, Myles New, Stuart Ovenden, Craig Robertson
Picture editor Carl Palmer

ACCOUNT MANAGEMENT
Publishing consultant Linda Swidenbank
Business director Andy Roughton
Group publishing director Kirsten Price

PRODUCTION
Production director Sophie Dillon
Colour reproduction by F1 Colour **Printed in Italy** by Rotolito Lombarda

Contents

Welcome to WW Kitchen Favourites

One of the great things about food is sharing – not just sharing a meal with friends or family, but also sharing your meal ideas, kitchen secrets and favourite recipes.

Whether it's posting your favourite food on Instagram, telling other members about that 'I-can't-believe-I-can-eat-this-on-Weight Watchers' recipe or just getting together with friends and talking about what you love to eat, there are lots of ways to share – and the Weight Watchers community makes it easy to connect with others.

In this book, we share with you some of the most popular recipes from the Weight Watchers recipe collection. With the help of our members, we've selected more than 60 meal ideas, desserts, snacks and even some drinks that have been tried, tested and loved.

From quick and easy midweek meals, to favourite family dishes and recipes that are perfect for entertaining, they don't just taste great, they are all low in SmartPoints too, so you can cook and enjoy them as part of your meal plan.

Plus you can find out from other members what it is that they love about the recipes in this book – we think you'll love them too.

Quick & easy

Time is precious, especially when juggling work and family life, so keeping meals speedy and simple is a must. Here's a selection of recipes that deliver plenty of flavour, fast!

"Food plays a central role in my life and has to be **delicious** at all times."
◄ LAURA

"I'm a busy **working mum**, so meals need to be **simple** and quick."
VICKY ►

"Working **shifts** can play havoc with your **eating habits**. Quick and easy solutions are a must."
CATHERINE ►

DEBBIE FENTON, MEMBER

Broccoli & Cheddar soup

Homemade soups are a brilliant idea if you're stuck for time – you can make a double batch and freeze some for later. This one is both flavoursome and filling, and makes a great lunch on a chilly day.

SERVES 4

PREP TIME
10 minutes

COOK TIME
30 minutes

Calorie controlled cooking spray
1 onion, chopped
2 garlic cloves, chopped
200g potatoes, peeled and
   chopped
1 litre vegetable stock, made
   with 1 stock cube

350g broccoli, broken into florets
   and stalk chopped
2-3 teaspoons wholegrain mustard
150g half-fat mature Cheddar,
   grated

1   Heat a large, nonstick pan and mist with cooking spray. Add the onion and garlic and cook, covered, for 3-4 minutes, until starting to soften. Stir in the potatoes and stock, then bring to the boil. Reduce the heat and simmer for 10 minutes.

2   Add the broccoli and simmer, covered, for 10 minutes until just tender. Remove from the heat, let it cool slightly and blend using a hand-held stick blender.

3   Return the pan to the heat, stir in the mustard and season with salt and freshly ground black pepper.

4   Warm through and serve topped with the grated Cheddar.

 SMARTPOINTS
5 per serving

✳   See page 6

> **"**
> Whenever there's a chill
> in the air, I make a big
> **batch of soup.** I love
> how indulgent this **cheesy
> version** tastes, yet it's still
> low in SmartPoints.
> **"**
> DEBBIE

LAURA MEYER, MEMBER & FOOD BLOGGER

Edamame salad

This is an easy accompaniment for burgers, sausages and grilled meat and is one of Laura's favourite low SmartPoints salads. Why not give it the taste test at your next barbecue?

SERVES 2

PREP TIME
5 minutes

Large handful mixed salad leaves
2 spring onions, finely sliced
2 small red peppers, deseeded
   and sliced
100g cucumber, sliced
100g cherry tomatoes, halved

2 tablespoons balsamic vinegar
65g shop-bought edamame
   and pea salad (use without
   the dressing)
25g light feta cheese, crumbled

1 In a bowl, toss together the salad leaves, spring onions, peppers, cucumber and cherry tomatoes. Drizzle over the balsamic vinegar.

2 Gently stir in the edamame salad and feta. Season with salt and freshly ground black pepper, then serve.

SMARTPOINTS
3 per serving

See page 6

> 66
> I like filling up
> on tasty salads
> at barbecues and
> then savouring
> my burger.
> 99
>
> LAURA

RACHEL CAMPBELL, MEMBER

Speedy spaghetti carbonara

This no-fuss carbonara is a firm favourite with lots of members, including Rachel and her twin sister, Aneka, who started cooking from scratch after joining Weight Watchers and lost 8st between them!

SERVES 4

PREP TIME
10 minutes

COOK TIME
15 minutes

300g spaghetti
Calorie controlled cooking spray
4 rashers back bacon, chopped
250g mushrooms, sliced
1 spring onion, finely chopped
1 garlic clove, halved

250g light soft cheese with herbs
1 egg
150ml skimmed milk
30g Parmesan cheese, grated
2 tablespoons chopped fresh
  flat-leaf parsley

1 Bring a large pan of lightly salted water to the boil. Add the spaghetti and cook for about 8 minutes, until al dente, or to pack instructions. Drain, reserving 100ml of the cooking water.

2 Meanwhile, heat a frying pan over a medium heat and mist with cooking spray. Add the bacon, mushrooms, spring onion and garlic, and cook for 5 minutes, until softened. Discard the garlic.

3 Beat the soft cheese and egg together in a mixing bowl, then add the bacon, mushrooms and spring onion mixture, stirring until combined. Add the milk, half the Parmesan and the parsley, then season. Put the pasta in a pan, stir in the egg mixture and heat gently for 2-3 minutes, stirring, until the mixture has cooked and thickened. Add a little of the reserved pasta water if the sauce is too thick.

4 Divide the spaghetti between four plates and serve topped with the remaining Parmesan.

SMARTPOINTS
15 per serving

66
This carbonara is so good – using light soft cheese instead of cream makes it healthier.
99
RACHEL

MELISSA VANZANT-BIRCH, MEMBER

Miso-grilled aubergines with sticky rice

This simple, Japanese-inspired veggie dish is ready in just half an hour. It's a favourite of lawyer Melissa, who regularly works 12-hour days and finds it tough to eat healthily throughout the week.

SERVES 2

PREP TIME
2 minutes

COOK TIME
30 minutes

2 aubergines
Calorie controlled cooking spray
150g sushi rice
2 tablespoons miso paste
2 tablespoons mirin
2 tablespoons sake

1 tablespoon caster sugar
100g green beans
2 tablespoons rice wine vinegar
1 tablespoon sesame seeds
2 spring onions, finely sliced

1   Preheat the oven to 180°C, fan 160°C, gas mark 4. Halve the aubergines and put them skin-side down on a baking tray, then score the flesh with a knife to make a diamond pattern. Mist with the cooking spray and bake for 25 minutes or until tender.

2   Meanwhile, put the rice in a pan with 200ml cold water. Cover and bring to the boil. Reduce the heat and simmer for 10 minutes. Remove from the heat and then leave to stand, covered, for another 10 minutes. The rice will absorb all the water so there is no need to drain.

3   Put the miso paste, mirin, sake and sugar in a small pan and bring to the boil. Once the aubergines are roasted, brush the miso mixture over them and grill for 2-3 minutes or until browned. Meanwhile, cook the green beans in boiling water for 2-3 minutes or until tender.

4   Stir the rice wine vinegar and sesame seeds into the rice and divide it between 2 plates. Serve with the aubergine halves, garnished with the green beans and sliced spring onions.

SMARTPOINTS
14 per serving

See page 6

> **"** I don't eat **meat** so it's great to find a filling, **speedy vegetarian** dish. **"**
>
> MELISSA

LUCY ELLINGTON & VICKY NEWMAN, MEMBERS

Prawn fajitas

Simple, healthy meals like these spicy Mexican-style prawn wraps are a must-have on everyone's meal plan. Friends Lucy and Vicky love making them when they get together for one of their girly weekends.

SERVES 4

PREP TIME
10 minutes

COOK TIME
12-15 minutes

1½ tablespoons fajita spice mix
300g raw peeled prawns
1 teaspoon olive oil
1 red onion, chopped
1 garlic clove, crushed
1 red and 1 yellow pepper,
  each deseeded and sliced
400g tin chopped tomatoes
8 corn tortillas

TO SERVE
Shredded iceberg lettuce
4 tablespoons low-fat soured cream
Red and green jalapeño peppers
Lime wedges

1 Toss the spice mix and prawns together and set aside to marinate until required. Heat the oil in a large frying pan, add the onion and cook for 3-4 minutes or until it begins to soften. Add the garlic and peppers and stir-fry for another 3 minutes. Add the tomatoes and cook over a medium heat until thickened.

2 Add the prawns to the sauce, cook through until pink and then season. To serve, arrange the lettuce, prawns and sauce on the tortillas, add the soured cream and jalapeños plus a squeeze of lime juice, then roll up and enjoy. Serve 2 fajitas per person.

SMARTPOINTS
Per serving 10

  See page 6

> **"** Neither of us are natural cooks, so we love how easy this recipe is. **"**
>
> LUCY

JAI DE'ATH, MEMBER

Cajun chicken salad

When time is short, this is a great go-to recipe. It's super tasty and any leftovers can be enjoyed the next day. You can even leave off the cheese to make it just 5 SmartPoints per serving.

SERVES 2

PREP TIME
10 minutes

COOK TIME
10 minutes

Calorie controlled cooking spray
2 x 165g skinless chicken breast fillets, flattened to a thickness of about 1cm
1 tablespoon Cajun seasoning
Juice of 1½ limes
40g Mexicana cheese, thinly sliced
40g mixed salad leaves
½ red onion, finely sliced

½ carrot, grated
1 courgette, peeled into ribbons
Handful cherry tomatoes, quartered
½ 198g tin sweetcorn, drained
2 tablespoons salsa
1 tablespoon reduced-fat soured cream
Small handful fresh coriander leaves, chopped

1 Preheat the grill to medium. Mist a nonstick griddle pan with the cooking spray and set over a medium heat. Mist the chicken with spray, then coat in the Cajun seasoning. Griddle for 3-4 minutes each side, until cooked through. Pour two-thirds of the lime juice onto the chicken, then top with the cheese. Put under the grill for 1-2 minutes, until the cheese has melted.

2 Meanwhile, toss the salad leaves, onion, carrot, courgette, tomatoes, sweetcorn and remaining lime juice in a large bowl. Top with the chicken and serve with the salsa, soured cream and coriander.

SMARTPOINTS
7 per serving

  See page 6

> 66
> This is so easy and the flavours work really well. It's great for a quick lunch when you're rushed for time.
> 99
> JAI

CATHERINE FOWLER, MEMBER

Salmon kedgeree

This speedy supper is ready in just 20 minutes. It's the perfect dish for Catherine, who works long shifts as a nurse and often struggles to find the time to cook healthy, sustaining meals.

SERVES 2

PREP TIME
5 minutes

COOK TIME
20 minutes

150g salmon fillet
1 egg
100g basmati rice
1 teaspoon sunflower oil
1 small onion, finely chopped
1 small garlic clove, chopped
2 teaspoons curry powder

1 teaspoon cumin seeds, lightly crushed
2 tomatoes, roughly chopped
3 tablespoons roughly chopped fresh coriander, plus extra leaves to garnish
1 lemon, cut into wedges

1 Preheat the grill to medium-high and grill the salmon for 10-15 minutes, turning occasionally, until cooked. Remove and allow to cool a little before removing and discarding the skin and roughly flaking the fish.

2 Meanwhile, boil the egg for 8 minutes, then cool under running water, peel and cut into quarters.

3 While the salmon and egg are cooking, rinse the rice well and put in a pan with plenty of water. Bring to the boil, then simmer gently until just tender. Tip into a sieve, cool under running water and drain well.

4 Heat the oil in a nonstick shallow pan, add the onion and gently cook for 5 minutes, adding a splash of water if it looks like it might catch. Add the chopped garlic, curry powder and cumin seeds and cook for 1 minute, or until fragrant.

5 Stir in the rice, season well and heat through until piping hot. Add the salmon, tomatoes and chopped coriander and combine well. Serve in warmed bowls and top with the quartered egg. Scatter the coriander leaves over and serve with the lemon wedges on the side.

SMARTPOINTS
11 per serving

 See page 6

“

I love how tasty
and **filling** this
is – it's a great
post-work dinner.

”

CATHERINE

Quick seafood pasta

This simple pasta dish is a favourite of WW food blogger, Laura (skinnykitchensecrets.com), whose recipes provide inspiration for her many followers. It's ready in less than 30 minutes.

SERVES 2

PREP TIME
10 minutes

COOK TIME
15 minutes

80g spaghetti
Calorie controlled cooking spray
1 onion, finely chopped
2 garlic cloves, finely chopped
1 red chilli, finely chopped (and deseeded if you don't like too much heat)
1½ teaspoons paprika
Pinch cayenne pepper
Pinch chilli powder

400g tin chopped tomatoes
100ml white wine
1 tablespoon tomato purée
½ teaspoon sugar
230g mixed cooked seafood, such as prawns, mussels and squid
2 tablespoons single cream
Handful fresh basil leaves, to garnish

1   Bring a large pan of water to the boil, add the spaghetti and cook for 10-12 minutes until al dente. Drain, reserving a splash of the pasta cooking water.

2   Meanwhile, heat a pan, mist with the cooking spray, then fry the onion, garlic and chilli over a medium heat for 5 minutes, until the onion has softened but not browned.

3   Add the paprika, cayenne pepper, chilli powder, tomatoes, wine, tomato purée and sugar to the pan, give it all a stir, and bring to the boil. Reduce the heat and simmer for another 5 minutes, stirring occasionally.

4   Stir in the seafood and cook for a further 3-4 minutes until the seafood is piping hot, then add the cream and warm through.

5   Add the cooked spaghetti and reserved pasta water to the sauce and stir until the pasta is well coated. Divide between bowls, serve garnished with the basil leaves and seasoned with freshly ground black pepper.

SMARTPOINTS
9 per serving

> I love this because it's packed full of flavour, and is incredibly quick to make.
>
> LAURA

NIGEL JOHNSON, MEMBER

Cheesy stuffed mushrooms

These are great as a meat-free lunch, served with a leafy green salad. You could add some chopped fresh herbs such as parsley or basil, if you like. Best of all, they're on the table in less than 30 minutes.

SERVES 4

PREP TIME
10 minutes

COOK TIME
18 minutes

Calorie controlled cooking spray
2 celery sticks, chopped
1 large carrot, chopped
2 onions, chopped

2 garlic cloves, crushed
4 large portobello mushrooms, stalks removed and chopped
160g Gruyère cheese, grated

1   Mist a frying pan with the cooking spray. Add the celery, carrot, onions, garlic and chopped mushroom stalks and cook, stirring, over a medium heat for 10 minutes until softened – add a little water if the mixture begins to stick. Season well with salt and freshly ground black pepper.

2   Preheat the grill to medium. Put the mushrooms on a baking tray, mist with cooking spray and grill for 5 minutes.

3   Top the mushrooms with the veg mixture and cheese, and grill for 2-3 minutes until the cheese is melted and bubbling. Serve seasoned with freshly ground black pepper.

SMARTPOINTS
6 per serving

See page 6

> 66
> I love these –
> they're **really easy**
> and make you look
> **creative** in the kitchen
> – which I'm not!
> 99
> NIGEL

FRANKIE WHIGHT, MEMBER

Italian sausage sandwich

This sausage sandwich has a spicy kick which makes it a great alternative to burgers and chicken drumsticks Barbecue fan Frankie and her family love this recipe.

SERVES 4

PREP TIME
10 minutes

COOK TIME
10-15 minutes

225g extra-lean sausages
8 x 25g slices ciabatta loaf, plus 25g for crumbs
¼ teaspoon fennel seeds
Pinch dried red chilli flakes
1 small sprig fresh oregano, finely chopped (or a pinch of dried)
Grated zest of ½ lemon

FOR THE SALAD
60g reduced-fat mozzarella ball, chopped
2 artichokes in brine, drained well and chopped
6 cherry tomatoes, sliced
Juice of 1 lemon
Few fresh basil leaves, shredded

1   Prepare your barbecue or, if you're cooking indoors, preheat the grill to medium. Squeeze the sausagemeat out of the sausages into a bowl. Make breadcrumbs from the 25g ciabatta and add it to the bowl with the fennel seeds, chilli flakes, oregano and lemon zest. Season with black pepper and mash together with a fork to blend, then shape into 4 short, fat sausages, cover and chill until needed.

2   Mix the salad ingredients together and season to taste. Cook your sausages on the barbecue for around 10 minutes, turning carefully, until done, or cook under the grill for 12-15 minutes. Toast the ciabatta lightly on the barbecue or under the grill. Top 4 slices of ciabatta with the salad, add a halved sausage to each, then top with the remaining ciabatta slices.

SMARTPOINTS
Per serving 7

> ❝
> I love how simply
> taking the cooking
> outside makes
> a meal so much
> more fun.
> ❞
>
> FRANKIE

NICOLA KIRK, WW PUBLISHING TEAM

Tuna pasta bake

Everyone loves a pasta bake, and this one is a real winner. Herbs, spices and extra veg add loads of flavour. You may already have most of the ingredients in your storecupboard.

SERVES 4

PREP TIME
10 minutes

COOK TIME
30-40 minutes

240g penne pasta
Calorie controlled cooking spray
2 onions, finely chopped
4 peppers, deseeded and sliced
3 garlic cloves, finely chopped
2 teaspoons paprika
2 teaspoons dried oregano
1 teaspoon chilli flakes

½ teaspoon cayenne pepper
400g tin tuna in water, drained
800g passata
2 teaspoons balsamic vinegar
Dash of Tabasco sauce
2 x 40g packs cheese sauce mix
40g reduced-fat mature Cheddar,
 finely grated

1 Preheat the oven to 180°C, fan 160°C, gas mark 4. Bring a pan of water to the boil and cook the pasta for 10-12 minutes, or to pack instructions, until tender, then drain.

2 Meanwhile, mist a large frying pan with the cooking spray, add the onions and peppers and cook over a medium heat for 5-10 minutes, or until softened. Add the garlic, paprika, oregano, chilli flakes and cayenne pepper and cook for 1 minute.

3 Stir in the tuna and season. Add the passata, balsamic vinegar and Tabasco sauce and bring to the boil. Reduce the heat and simmer for 2-3 minutes. Remove from the heat and stir in the cooked pasta.

4 Combine the cheese sauce mix with 250ml boiling water in a jug and stir until thickened. Gently stir into the pasta mixture, then spoon into 4 individual pie dishes or a 2 litre baking dish. Top with the grated cheese and bake for 20-25 minutes, until the cheese is melted and golden.

SMARTPOINTS
12 per serving

> "This has become one of my **stand-by** recipes. I love that it's a little bit spicy, and the **peppers** are a really nice addition."
>
> NICOLA

Yogurt dressing

This zesty, smoky dressing adds an instant burst of flavour. Try it with a mix of leafy greens, avocado and tomato, or with a chickpea, lentil and quinoa salad.

SERVES 4

PREP TIME
5 minutes

Whisk together 100g **0% fat natural Greek yogurt** with 2 tablespoons **lemon juice**, a pinch of **smoked paprika** and a small finely chopped **garlic clove**. Season to taste and serve with a sprinkling of paprika.

SMARTPOINTS 0 per serving

Dressings & sauces

Try food editor Sarah's favourite quick and easy ways to liven up salads and grilled meats.

Thai dressing

This will add an instant kick to poached chicken or turkey breast. It's also great with cooked rice noodles tossed with shredded carrots, cucumber, mange tout, bean sprouts and toasted cashew nuts.

SERVES 4

PREP TIME
5 minutes

Whisk the juice of 1 **lime** together with 1 tablespoon **fish sauce**, 2 tablespoons **rice vinegar**, 1 teaspoon **sugar** and 1 deseeded and finely chopped **red chilli**, then serve.

SMARTPOINTS
1 per serving

Soy & ginger dressing

This dressing is great with oily fish, such as salmon, or pair it with fried rice and stir-fried veggies for a quick and healthy Asian supper.

SERVES 4

PREP TIME
5 minutes

COOK TIME
3 minutes

Heat 1 tablespoon **groundnut oil** in a small pan, then add a 1cm-piece of fresh grated **ginger** and a small crushed **garlic clove**. Cook for 1 minute, then add 2 tablespoons **soy sauce**, 1 tablespoon **rice vinegar**, 1 tablespoon **clear honey** and ¼ teaspoon **Chinese five spice**. Simmer for 2 minutes, then serve.

SMARTPOINTS
3 per serving

Honey & mustard sauce

Great with roast chicken and pork, or roasted vegetables such as aubergines, courgettes, tomatoes and red onions.

SERVES 4

PREP TIME
5 minutes

COOK TIME
5 minutes

Melt 3 tablespoons **low-fat olive oil spread** in a small pan, then add 1½ tablespoons white wine **vinegar**, 1 tablespoon **Dijon mustard** and 2 teaspoons **clear honey**. Combine ½ teaspoon **cornflour** with 1½ tablespoons water and add to the pan. Bring to the boil, then simmer for 1-2 minutes, or until slightly thickened. Season to taste and serve.

SMARTPOINTS 3 per serving

Creamy white wine dressing

Serve with white fish, such as sea bass, bream or haddock. It's also great with leftover roast chicken.

MAKES 4

PREP TIME
5 minutes

COOK TIME
20 minutes

Heat a small pan over a medium-low heat and mist with **calorie controlled cooking spray**. Add 1 finely chopped **shallot** and cook for 5 minutes, until softened. Add 75ml **white wine**, bring to the boil, then simmer for 5-6 minutes, or until reduced by two-thirds. Add 150ml **vegetable stock**, made with half a **stock cube**, and 3 tablespoons **single cream**, and stir to combine. Simmer gently for 10 minutes, or until thickened. Season to taste and stir in 1 tablespoon chopped fresh **chives**, then serve.

SMARTPOINTS 2 per serving

> ❝
> Learn how to whip up these punchy, flavourful sauces and you'll always be able to create a delicious meal.
> ❞

SARAH FROM THE
WW KITCHEN TEAM

*See page 6

Family favourites

Midweek mealtimes can be a challenge when there are fussy eaters in the house. Try these quick, tasty and healthy recipes, that will keep everyone happy.

"We want meals that are **filling** and packed with **flavour.**"
◀ LOUISE

"The recipes are so **easy** and **tasty**, they've **inspired me** to start **experimenting** in the kitchen."
HOLLY ▶

"I'm looking for quick and easy **meal solutions** that will suit everyone."
◀ TANYA

SARAH O'NEILL, MEMBER

Lasagne

Who doesn't love lasagne? Sarah loves that the aubergine in this healthier version really beefs up the dish, and you can even save time by making the meat sauce a couple of days before assembling it.

SERVES 6

PREP TIME
15 minutes

COOK TIME
3 hours
5 minutes

1 aubergine
2 teaspoons olive oil
1 onion, diced
2 celery sticks, diced
2 carrots, diced
500g extra-lean beef mince
4 garlic cloves, chopped
100g sun-dried tomato pesto

400g tin chopped tomatoes
1 tablespoon low-fat spread
1 tablespoon plain flour
300ml skimmed milk
60g half-fat mature
   Cheddar cheese, grated
9 dried lasagne sheets
15g Parmesan cheese, grated

1 Preheat the oven to 200°C, fan 180°C, gas mark 6. Wrap the aubergine in foil and bake for 1 hour 30 minutes until soft. Chop into 1cm cubes.

2 Heat the oil in a large pan and cook the onion, celery and carrots for 15 minutes. Add the mince and garlic. Brown the mince, then add the aubergine, pesto, tomatoes and a tin of water, and simmer for 30 minutes.

3 Reduce the oven to 190°C, fan 170°C, gas mark 5. Gently heat the low-fat spread, flour and milk in a pan until bubbling. Simmer for 5 minutes, add two-thirds of the Cheddar and season.

4 In an ovenproof dish, top a third of the meat sauce with 3 lasagne sheets, then a third of the cheese sauce. Repeat with remaining sauces and pasta. Scatter over the Parmesan and remaining Cheddar. Bake for 45-50 minutes, then serve.

SMARTPOINTS
10 per serving

"
This is a **fantastic** lasagne. A foodie friend couldn't believe it's a **Weight Watchers** recipe. We love it!'
"
SARAH

TANYA MCMILLAN, MEMBER

Fish finger soft tacos

These tacos are perfect for mum Tanya, who loves to cook meals from scratch when she can. It's a great recipe for the kids to get involved in.

SERVES 5

PREP TIME
25 minutes

COOK TIME
25 minutes

4 slices calorie controlled white bread
1 tablespoon plain flour
1 egg, beaten
300g skinless pollock fillets, sliced into finger-length strips
Calorie controlled cooking spray
5 soft tortilla wraps
100g red cabbage, shredded, to serve
100g low-fat natural yogurt, to serve
Pinch of paprika, to serve

FOR THE SWEETCORN SALSA
198g tin sweetcorn, drained
½ small red onion, finely diced
75g cucumber, deseeded and diced
1 red chilli, deseeded and finely chopped (adjust to taste)
Small handful fresh coriander leaves, roughly chopped
Finely grated zest and juice of 1 lime

1 Combine the salsa ingredients, season and set aside. The salsa will keep, covered, in the fridge for 24 hours.

2 Blitz the bread in a food processor to make breadcrumbs and sprinkle them on a plate. Sprinkle the flour on a separate plate and pour the egg into a shallow bowl.

3 Preheat the oven to 180°C, fan 160°C, gas mark 4. Dip the strips of pollock in the flour, then the egg and then the breadcrumbs. Arrange on a baking tray misted with cooking spray and bake for 25 minutes or until golden.

4 Meanwhile, grill the tortillas for 2–3 minutes or until browned and starting to crisp up. Top each tortilla with a handful of cabbage, some sweetcorn salsa, a couple of fish fingers, a spoonful of yogurt and a pinch of paprika. The tortillas can either be served open (grill them for a few minutes longer to ensure they are extra crispy) or folded up.

SMARTPOINTS
8 per serving

> **"**
> These really suit us in our house – they're **nutritious** and **everyone's happy** to have them served up at dinner time.
> **"**
>
> TANYA

SAMANTHA REES, WW PUBLISHING TEAM

Fish pie with cauliflower mash

This fish pie with a twist has a cauliflower topping, which adds a lot of flavour to the dish. Piping the topping onto the pie makes it look extra special.

SERVES 4

PREP TIME
20 minutes

COOK TIME
50 minutes

1 extra-large cauliflower, broken into florets (around 750g)
2 tablespoons half-fat crème fraîche
15g unsalted butter
1 tablespoon plain flour
300ml semi-skimmed milk
2 teaspoons wholegrain mustard

200g young leaf spinach
300g smoked haddock fillet, cut into large chunks
250g skinless salmon fillet, cut into large chunks
15g Parmesan cheese, grated

1 Cook the cauliflower in a large pan of boiling water for 8-10 minutes, or until completely tender. Drain and set aside in a colander for a few minutes to steam-dry. Transfer to a food processor with the crème fraîche and blitz to a purée. Season and set aside.

2 To make a white sauce, heat the butter in a frying pan over a medium heat until frothy. Add the flour and stir well to make a paste. Cook over a low heat for 2 minutes, then gradually add the milk, stirring well between each addition, until you have a smooth sauce. Simmer gently for a few minutes, until the sauce thickens. Add the mustard, and season well.

3 Preheat the oven to 200°C, fan 180°C, gas mark 6. Wilt the spinach briefly in the microwave, then squeeze out as much water as possible and add to the sauce, along with the fish. Transfer to a 20cm x 26cm pie dish.

4 Top with the cauliflower mash, either piping it on in swirls using a piping bag fitted with a star nozzle or forking over the surface to create a rough texture. Scatter over the Parmesan and bake for 20-25 minutes, then finish it off under a hot grill for 5 minutes to get a crisp, golden crust.

5 Serve with some zero SmartPoints green vegetables on the side.

 SMARTPOINTS
9 per serving

> **This is a brilliant family dish – it looks and tastes amazing and couldn't be easier to make.**
>
> SAMANTHA

GRAHAM KING & ANDY HENDERSON, MEMBERS

Chilli con carne

This chilli has loads of flavour and is served with brown rice to make it healthier. It became a favourite of Graham and his partner Andy, and helped them lose more than 18 stone between them!

SERVES 4

PREP TIME
10 minutes

COOK TIME
45 minutes

Calorie controlled cooking spray
450g lean steak mince
1 onion, finely chopped
2 garlic cloves, crushed
1 red pepper, deseeded
  and roughly chopped
½-1 tablespoon mild chilli
  powder, plus a pinch to garnish
1 teaspoon ground cumin

400g tin chopped tomatoes
½ x 400g tin red kidney
  beans, drained and rinsed
250ml beef stock, made with
  1 stock cube
240g brown rice
4 tablespoons low-fat natural
  yogurt, to serve
Fresh coriander leaves, to garnish

1 Heat a large pan over a medium heat. When hot, mist with the cooking spray and add the mince. Turn the heat to high and cook for 5 minutes, stirring, until the mince is browned.

2 Stir in the onion, garlic and pepper, and cook for 5 minutes more, until the onion has started to soften. Add the chilli powder (depending how spicy you like it) and all of the cumin, then cook for 1 minute.

3 Add the tomatoes, red kidney beans and beef stock to the pan, stir, then season to taste. Reduce to a simmer, cover and cook for 30 minutes, stirring occasionally.

4 Meanwhile, cook the rice to pack instructions, then drain.

5 Serve the chilli and rice topped with a spoonful of yogurt and garnished with the coriander and extra chilli powder. The chilli can be frozen, without the rice, coriander and yogurt.

SMARTPOINTS
11 per serving

See page 6

“
We love having this
on an **evening in,**
but these days it's
without a second
portion.
”
ANDY

CAROLINE KULEMEKA, MEMBER

Easy roast chicken dinner

This one-dish roast dinner is easy to prepare and is on the table in an hour. No-fuss midweek dinners like this are a lifesaver if, like Caroline, you don't want to spend ages in the kitchen.

SERVES 5

PREP TIME
10 minutes

COOK TIME
50 minutes

200ml chicken stock made with ½ stock cube
1 tablespoon wholegrain mustard
Pared zest and juice of 1 lemon
2 garlic cloves, crushed
10 chicken drumsticks, skin removed
800g new potatoes, halved

300g baby carrots, scrubbed and halved
1 tablespoon clear honey
200g green beans
Fresh sage leaves, chopped, to garnish

1 Preheat the oven to 200°C, fan 180°C, gas mark 6. Mix together the chicken stock, mustard, lemon zest, juice and garlic and set aside.

2 Arrange the chicken drumsticks in a large roasting tin or 2 medium roasting tins (don't crowd the tins too much). Tuck the potatoes and carrots in between the drumsticks. Pour the chicken stock mixture over all of the ingredients, then drizzle the honey over the chicken.

3 Roast for 30 minutes. Add the green beans to the pan and roast for a further 20 minutes. Serve garnished with the chopped sage.

SMARTPOINTS
6 per serving

GF See page 6

> " This is great if you're **cooking** for a crowd. Everything goes into **one pan** then into the oven. Simple! "
> CAROLINE

HOLLY KINNAIRD, MEMBER

Thai fried rice

This fried rice dish is a winner! Holly told us that having lots of quick, easy dinner recipes like this meant she'd be less likely to fall back into old habits.

SERVES 4

PREP TIME
10 minutes

COOK TIME
10 minutes

4 small eggs
2 teaspoons fish sauce
Calorie controlled cooking spray
2 small onions, cut into thin wedges
2 carrots, cut into matchsticks
180g fine green beans, cut into short lengths
400g skinless chicken breast fillet, sliced

80g Thai red curry paste
400g cooked rice (brown or white)

TO SERVE
Sliced cucumber
Chopped fresh coriander
Lime wedges

1   Beat the eggs and fish sauce together in a bowl. Heat a wok until very hot, then mist with the cooking spray. Add the egg mixture and swirl around the pan. Cook briefly to set, then flip over using a spatula to seal the other side. Transfer to a plate and slice the omelette into ribbons.

2   Mist the wok with cooking spray again and add the vegetables. Stir-fry for 2 minutes, then push to one side, mist the exposed half of the pan with more spray and add the chicken pieces. Stir-fry the chicken for 2 minutes or until browned, then stir into the vegetables and stir-fry the whole lot for another minute.

3   Add the curry paste and 1 tablespoon water, stir to combine, then stir in the cooked rice. Cook for a further 1-2 minutes, then check that the chicken is cooked through. Spoon into a shallow bowl, top with the omelette ribbons, cucumber and coriander, and serve with lime wedges.

SMARTPOINTS
8 per serving

See page 6

66

I love this fried rice with omelette strips. It's so easy and tasty, it inspired me to start experimenting in the kitchen.

99

HOLLY

LOUISE TOMPKINS, MEMBER & FOOD BLOGGER

Grilled chicken with pesto pasta

This simple, tasty pasta dish is a big favourite for Louise, who set up an Instagram account (@lou_wwgoldmember) at the beginning of her weight loss journey and now has thousands of followers, thanks to her brilliant recipes.

SERVES 4

PREP TIME
5 minutes
+ cooling

COOK TIME
15 minutes

600g skinless chicken breast fillets
260g wholewheat fusilli
24 cherry tomatoes, halved
4 tablespoons reduced-fat
   green pesto
Large handful fresh basil leaves,
   to garnish

1   Preheat the grill to medium-high. Season the chicken and grill for 15 minutes, turning once, until cooked through. Set aside to cool slightly, then slice into bite-size pieces.

2   Meanwhile, cook the pasta to pack instructions, then drain.

3   Combine the chicken, cooked pasta, tomatoes and pesto in serving bowls. Garnish with the basil leaves to serve.

SMARTPOINTS
9 per serving

“
This chicken
pasta is filling
and packed
full of flavour.
”
LOUISE

JULIA WESTGARTH, WW PROGRAMME TEAM

Veggie mac 'n' cheese

An easy pasta bake that tastes delicious and, by using broccoli and cauliflower instead of just pasta, is lower in SmartPoints too!

SERVES 4

PREP TIME
10 minutes

COOK TIME
15 minutes

200g fresh penne pasta
150g each of cauliflower and
   broccoli, cut into small florets
40g pack Cheddar
   cheese sauce mix

400ml semi-skimmed milk
1 teaspoon wholegrain mustard
2 tomatoes, sliced

1   Bring a pan of water to the boil and cook the pasta, cauliflower and broccoli for 5-6 minutes, then drain.

2   Meanwhile, preheat the grill to medium-high. Put the sauce mix in a pan and whisk in a little of the milk. Stir in the remaining milk and bring to the boil, stirring. Reduce the heat and simmer for 2 minutes until thickened, then stir in the mustard. Season with black pepper.

3   Transfer the pasta and veg to an ovenproof dish, pour the sauce over and stir. Top with the tomatoes and grill for 5 minutes, until the top begins to brown.

SMARTPOINTS
6 per serving

> I love this mac 'n' cheese – it's so quick and easy to make, and tastes great.
>
> JULIA

EMMA HOLLAND, MEMBER

Aubergine parmigiana

This classic Italian-style bake tastes amazing, is easy to make, and is budget-friendly too, so it ticked all the boxes for Emma. You could also make it with grilled courgettes, instead of aubergine.

SERVES 2

PREP TIME
10 minutes

COOK TIME
35 minutes

2 aubergines, sliced lengthways
Calorie controlled cooking spray
1 garlic clove
350g jar low-fat tomato and basil
  pasta sauce

2 tablespoons fresh white
  breadcrumbs
2 tablespoons vegetarian hard
  Italian cheese, grated
Fresh basil leaves, to serve

1 Preheat the grill. Put the aubergine slices on a baking sheet and mist with cooking spray. Grill for 2-3 minutes on each side, until softened.

2 Preheat the oven to 190°C, fan 170°C, gas mark 5. Rub the garlic clove around the insides of two individual gratin dishes (or 1 larger one). Spoon half the pasta sauce into the base of the dishes. Arrange the grilled aubergine on top, season, then spoon the rest of the pasta sauce over them.

3 Mix together the breadcrumbs and the Parmesan, then sprinkle evenly over the surface of each dish. Bake for 20-25 minutes or until the parmigiana is golden and bubbling. Serve scattered with the fresh basil leaves.

SMARTPOINTS
5 per serving

> ❝ This is a brilliant veggie dish that's **healthy** and delicious – and it's good for the **finances** too. ❞
>
> EMMA

DEE EDGAR, MEMBER

Cottage pie

This is a classic dinnertime dish with a twist – lentils and lots of fresh vegetables. Cottage pie is a big family favourite in Dee's house – everyone loves it!

SERVES 4

PREP TIME
15 minutes

COOK TIME
1-1 hour
15 minutes
+ standing

Calorie controlled cooking spray
1 onion, diced
1 carrot, diced
1 celery stick, diced
2 garlic cloves, chopped finely
200g extra-lean minced beef
40g dried red lentils
½ small courgette, grated

400g tin chopped tomatoes
400ml beef stock made with
 ½ stock cube
2 teaspoons tomato ketchup
2 teaspoons Worcestershire sauce
800g potatoes, cut into chunks
1 tablespoon low-fat spread
2 tablespoons skimmed milk

1 Heat a nonstick pan, mist with the cooking spray and add the onion, carrot and celery. Cook for 4–5 minutes, then add the garlic and mince. Cook for 3-4 minutes to brown the mince. Stir in the lentils and courgette.

2 Add the tomatoes, stock, ketchup and Worcestershire sauce. Season, then simmer for 20–25 minutes or until the lentils are cooked. Pour into a pie dish.

3 Meanwhile, cook the potatoes in boiling water until tender, then drain and mash with the spread and milk and season. Put dollops of mashed potato around the edge of the pie and push into the centre using a fork, so that the whole pie surface is covered.

4 Preheat the oven to 190ºC, fan 170ºC, gas mark 5 and bake the pie for 30-40 minutes or until the top is brown and the sauce is bubbling. Stand for 5 minutes, then serve with green vegetables. The pie can be frozen for up to 1 month. Defrost in the fridge overnight before cooking as in step 4.

SMARTPOINTS
8 per serving

  See page 6

" I enjoy classic comfort food and use as many fresh ingredients as possible. "

DEE

HOLLY KINNAIRD, MEMBER

Sausage, tomato & herb risotto

This all-in-one risotto is on the table in just 35 minutes, so it's perfect for busy mum Holly. She's always on the lookout for meal ideas that are quick, taste great and appeal to the whole family.

SERVES 4

PREP TIME
5 minutes

COOK TIME
30 minutes

2 teaspoons low-fat spread
2 shallots or ½ onion, diced
125g risotto rice
40ml dry white wine
500ml chicken or vegetable
   stock made with ½ cube

Calorie controlled cooking spray
3 extra-lean pork sausages
12 cherry tomatoes on the vine
A few fresh chives, snipped

1   Preheat the oven to 200°C, fan 180°C, gas mark 6. Melt the low-fat spread in a pan, add the shallots or onion and cook gently for 5 minutes or until softened. Add the rice and stir for 1 minute, then add the wine and let it sizzle away for around 30 seconds. Start adding the hot stock, bit by bit, stirring all the while, until the liquid is all absorbed and the rice is plumped up and creamy.

2   Meanwhile, line a shallow roasting tray with baking paper and mist with cooking spray. Squeeze the sausagemeat from the sausage skins directly onto the paper to make 15–18 balls. Mist with more spray and roast for 15 minutes, then turn and add the tomatoes to the tray and cook for a further 10 minutes or until the sausage balls are cooked through and golden and the tomatoes are bursting.

3   Pull the tomatoes from the vine and stir them and the sausage balls into the cooked risotto. Season to taste and sprinkle over the chives to serve.

SMARTPOINTS
6 per serving

> "We are all so **hungry** when we get home that I have to get **food** in front of them **fast**. This **risotto** always goes down well."

HOLLY

Three-in-one dips with crudités

These easy yogurt-based dips make a great family-friendly snack. Adjust the spiciness to keep everyone happy.

MAKES 3 DIPS

PREP TIME
15 minutes

For the harissa dip, put 250g **0% fat natural Greek yogurt** in a bowl and add 2 tablespoons **harissa paste**. Season well and stir to combine. For the cucumber and mint dip, put 250g **0% fat natural Greek yogurt** in a bowl, then add half a finely diced **cucumber** and a handful of **fresh mint**, finely chopped. Season well and stir. For the basil and lemon dip, put the 250g **0% fat natural Greek yogurt** in a mini processor with a handful of **fresh basil** leaves, roughly chopped, and the juice of half a **lemon**. Blitz until you have a smooth consistency. Season well and transfer to a bowl. Sprinkle with lemon zest to finish. Serve the dips in little pots, garnished with sprigs of **herbs** and **crudités** for dunking.

Harissa dip
SMARTPOINTS 4 per pot

Cucumber & mint dip
SMARTPOINTS 3 per pot

Basil & lemon dip
SMARTPOINTS 3 per pot

Basil & lemon dip

Spiced tacos

SERVES 6

PREP TIME
5 minutes

COOK TIME
7 minutes

Preheat the oven to 200°C, fan 180°C, gas mark 6. Tear 2 **Weight Watchers Wraps** into bite-size pieces, spread over a nonstick baking sheet and mist with **calorie controlled cooking spray**. Sprinkle with smoked **paprika** and **chilli powder** to taste, and season well. Using your fingers, turn the pieces of wrap to coat them in the spices. Bake for 5 minutes, then turn over and bake for another 2 minutes until golden and crisp. Serve straight away.

SMARTPOINTS 1 per serving

> 66
> We love these dips in our house. They're a brilliant **healthy snack** to fill in the gaps between mealtimes – and the crudités help you sneak in **more veg** for kids.
>
> NADINE FROM THE WW KITCHEN TEAM
> 99

Harissa dip

Cucumber & mint dip

Tip
Carrots, celery, cucumber, peppers and mange tout are all great for crudités.

*See page 6

Food for friends

Summer barbecues, special celebrations or a lazy lunch with friends – sharing food with the people you love makes it taste that much better...

"I tend to **make** things that can be done in **one pan** – it makes life a lot easier."
◀ SAMANTHA

"If something **looks good**, it immediately makes me want to **try it**."
◀ LAVON

"It's wonderful knowing that we can have a **great time** and still maintain our **goal weights**."
JAN ▶

NICOLE MILTON, MEMBER

Moroccan fish tagine with lemon couscous

This colourful dish looks impressive and tastes extra special, which makes it ideal for entertaining – and it's ready in just 30 minutes!

SERVES 4

PREP TIME 10 minutes

COOK TIME 20 minutes

Calorie controlled cooking spray
1 onion, finely sliced
1 red and 1 green pepper, each deseeded and finely sliced
2 garlic cloves, finely sliced
1 tablespoon harissa paste
1 cinnamon stick
200g tin chopped tomatoes
200ml vegetable stock, made with ½ cube
50g dried apricots, sliced

600g skinless cod fillets, cut into large chunks
Handful fresh coriander leaves, to serve

FOR THE COUSCOUS
200g couscous
200ml hot vegetable stock, made with 1 cube
Grated zest and juice of ½ lemon

1 Mist a large, nonstick, lidded frying pan with the cooking spray. Add the onion and peppers and fry for 5 minutes until softened, adding a splash of water if necessary to prevent them burning. Add the garlic and harissa paste, then cook for 2-3 minutes.

2 Stir in the cinnamon, tomatoes, stock and apricots. Bring to the boil, then reduce the heat and simmer for 5 minutes. Season to taste.

3 Stir in the cod, cover, and simmer for 5 minutes until the fish is just cooked. Discard the cinnamon.

4 Meanwhile, prepare the couscous. Put it in a heatproof bowl, pour over the stock, cover with cling film and let stand for 5 minutes until the liquid has been absorbed. Fluff up the grains with a fork and stir in the lemon zest and juice.

5 Sprinkle the coriander over the tagine, then serve with the couscous.

 SMARTPOINTS
8 per serving

> " We eat fish a lot at home because it's great to fill up on. I love that this recipe uses couscous, as it's so quick and easy. "
>
> NICOLE

NIKKI SIMPSON, MEMBER

Prawn & fish burgers

Try these as a delicious alternative to meat-based burgers at your next barbecue. You can use any kind of white fish fillets you like.

MAKES 4

PREP TIME
15 minutes +
chilling

COOK TIME
20 minutes

250g firm white fish fillets, such as cod, chopped
300g raw peeled prawns, roughly chopped
5 spring onions, trimmed and roughly chopped
2 tablespoons chopped fresh flat-leaf parsley
50g fresh white breadcrumbs
Juice of ½ lemon
40g reduced-fat mayonnaise
1 tablespoon olive oil
4 x 60g sesame seed topped burger buns or rolls, toasted

Lettuce, sliced tomatoes and cucumber ribbons, to serve

FOR THE AVOCADO AÏOLI
1 avocado, peeled, stone removed and flesh mashed
1 garlic clove, finely chopped
20g reduced-fat mayonnaise
1 tablespoon chopped fresh coriander
1 green chilli, deseeded and finely chopped
Juice of 1 lime

1   Put the fish, prawns, spring onions, parsley, breadcrumbs, lemon juice and mayonnaise into a food processor. Season and pulse until just combined. Shape into 4 patties, then chill for 30 minutes.

2   Heat a nonstick griddle or frying pan to medium, brush the burgers with the oil and cook for 4-5 minutes each side, or until golden. Reduce the heat to low and cook for a further 5 minutes on each side.

3   Meanwhile, make the aïoli. Mix the avocado with the garlic, mayonnaise, coriander and chilli. Stir in the lime juice and season to taste.

4   To serve, fill the toasted buns with lettuce and tomatoes, followed by the fish burgers, cucumber and avocado aïoli.

SMARTPOINTS
12 per burger

> "These are incredibly **simple** to create and very tasty. For a 12 SmartPoints meal, they are a **real treat!**"
>
> NIKKI

LAVON HENDRICKS, MEMBER

Turkey larb bites

This Thai-inspired dish is spicy and full of flavour.
It's perfect for sharing and a favourite of Lavon's –
she says she became much more adventurous in
the kitchen after joining Weight Watchers.

SERVES 4

PREP TIME
15 minutes

COOK TIME
15 minutes

2 tablespoons Thai jasmine rice
Calorie controlled cooking spray
1 banana shallot, finely chopped
2 garlic cloves, finely sliced
1 teaspoon lemongrass paste
500g turkey breast mince
Juice of 1 lime, plus extra
  wedges to serve
1 tablespoon fish sauce

½ tablespoon palm sugar
1 red bird's-eye chilli, finely sliced
6 spring onions, trimmed and
  sliced on the diagonal
Handful each fresh coriander and
  fresh mint leaves, chopped
12 Little Gem lettuce leaves

1   Heat a small nonstick frying pan over a high heat and toast the rice for
4-5 minutes until golden brown. Transfer to a pestle and mortar and crush
to a fine powder.

2   Mist a large nonstick frying pan with the cooking spray and cook the shallot
over a medium heat for 3-4 minutes, until soft. Add the garlic and lemongrass
paste and continue to cook for 1 minute, before adding the turkey. Cook over a
medium heat for 5 minutes until the turkey is browned. Remove from the heat
and set aside.

3   In a small bowl, mix together the lime juice, fish sauce and palm sugar until the
sugar has dissolved. Pour the dressing over the turkey mixture, add the chilli,
spring onions, herbs and toasted rice, and mix well to combine.

4   Spoon the larb mixture into the lettuce cups and serve with the lime wedges
for squeezing over.

SMARTPOINTS
4 per serving

See page 6

> ## "
> I was inspired by the
> Thai food that I
> found on Instagram.
> I love that it's so
> healthy but is also
> packed with flavour.
> ## "
>
> LAVON

JOHN CAMPBELL, MEMBER

Provençal beef

Hearty and warming, this fuss-free, French-style casserole is a favourite dish of John's, who lost 6st on his weight loss journey and was one of the winners of our Weight Watchers Awards.

SERVES 6

PREP TIME 15 minutes

COOK TIME 6-7 hours

Calorie controlled cooking spray
1 onion, chopped
300g button mushrooms, halved
2 garlic cloves, crushed
2 carrots, sliced into rounds
450g lean beef stewing steak, cut into small chunks
400g tin pinto beans, drained and rinsed

350ml vegetable stock, made with 1 cube
400g tin chopped tomatoes
½ teaspoon salt
½ teaspoon dried oregano
¼ teaspoon dried thyme
¼ teaspoon freshly ground black pepper
Fresh thyme sprigs, to garnish

1   Mist a nonstick frying pan with cooking spray and cook the onion, mushrooms and garlic over a medium-high heat for 5 minutes, stirring occasionally. Transfer to a slow cooker with the carrots, beef and half the beans.

2   Put the remaining beans in a food processor with one third of the vegetable stock and blitz until smooth. Add to the slow cooker with the remaining stock, tomatoes, salt, dried herbs and pepper.

3   Cover and cook on high for 6-7 hours, until the beef and veg are tender. If you don't have a slow cooker, cook in a covered casserole dish in the oven at 160°C, fan 140°C, gas mark 3 for 1 hour 30 minutes. Serve the stew garnished with the fresh thyme.

SMARTPOINTS
4 per serving

GF   See page 6

> "
> My mum used to make **beef stew** when I was little, so this brings back **wonderful** food memories.
> "
>
> JOHN

JAN PARRIS, MEMBER

Stuffed chicken breasts with mushrooms & Stilton

This impressive-looking and delicious chicken dish was a big hit with Jan and her daughter Elaine who lost more than 4st between them and wanted to celebrate their weight-loss success with a special meal.

SERVES 2

PREP TIME
10 minutes

COOK TIME
25 minutes

- 10g dried wild mushrooms
- 30g Stilton cheese, finely chopped
- 2 x 150g skinless chicken breasts
- 6 thin slices of pancetta (42g)
- Calorie controlled cooking spray
- 150g baby carrots
- 2 teaspoons low-fat spread
- ½ teaspoon light brown soft sugar
- 235g young leaf spinach
- 50ml Champagne, cava or sparkling white wine
- 25ml double cream
- Snipped fresh chives

1   Preheat the oven to 200°C, fan 180°C, gas mark 6. Put the dried mushrooms in a small heatproof bowl and cover with boiling water. Leave for 10 minutes, drain, then squeeze out the excess water and chop finely. Mix with the chopped Stilton and a little black pepper.

2   Cut a slit down the side of each chicken fillet to make a pocket. Stuff with the mushroom mixture, then wrap each fillet in 3 slices of pancetta. Mist a small flame-proof baking dish with cooking spray and put the chicken parcels in it, then mist the tops of the parcels with cooking spray. Cook in the oven for 20 minutes or until cooked through.

3   Meanwhile, steam the baby carrots for 3 minutes or until just tender. Melt the spread in a pan, add the carrots, the sugar and some seasoning. Cover and cook for 2-3 minutes or until glossy. Transfer to a warm serving bowl, then wilt the spinach in the same pan.

4   Divide the vegetables between 2 plates and top with the chicken. Put the baking dish with its juices over a medium heat, add the Champagne and let it bubble for a minute or so, then stir in the cream and chives. Season to taste and warm through. Spoon the sauce over the chicken to serve.

SMARTPOINTS
12 per serving

GF   See page 6

> Cooking is a **passion** of mine – I'm always trying to make my **favourite** recipes lower in SmartPoints.

JAN

IMOGEN PRESCOTT, WW PUBLISHING TEAM

Mushroom & lentil burgers

Summer get-togethers are a great chance to enjoy healthy, delicious food with friends. This flavour-packed veggie burger is perfect for grilling.

MAKES 4

PREP TIME
20 minutes +
chilling

COOK TIME
30 minutes

15g dried mixed mushrooms
3 teaspoons olive oil
1 onion, finely chopped
300g fresh mushrooms, chopped
2 garlic cloves, finely chopped
6 sprigs fresh thyme, leaves picked
   and chopped
2 tablespoons chopped fresh
   flat-leaf parsley
175g cooked green lentils, drained
15g vegetarian Italian hard
   cheese, grated

1 teaspoon English mustard
20g walnuts, finely chopped
2 tablespoons plain flour
4 x 60g wholemeal burger buns
Lettuce, sliced tomatoes and
   cress, to serve

FOR THE SALAD
100g frozen or fresh broad beans
100g frozen or fresh petits pois
25g light feta cheese, crumbled
35g 0% fat natural Greek yogurt

1   Put the dried mushrooms in a small heatproof bowl, cover with boiling water and leave for 10-15 minutes. Drain and chop.

2   Heat 1 teaspoon of the oil in a pan and cook the onion for 5 minutes. Add the fresh mushrooms and cook for 5-10 minutes, until any water has evaporated. Add the garlic and herbs and cook for 3 minutes. Tip into a bowl.

3   Stir the rehydrated mushrooms, lentils, cheese, mustard and walnuts into the mushroom mixture and season to taste. In a food processor, whizz half the mixture to a purée, then combine with the rest of the mixture and the flour. Shape into 4 patties and chill for 30 minutes.

4   Heat a nonstick griddle or frying pan to medium, brush the patties with the remaining oil and cook for 3-4 minutes each side. Reduce the heat to low and cook the burgers for a further 5 minutes on each side.

5   Meanwhile, bring a pan of water to the boil. Add the broad beans and petits pois and cook for 2 minutes. Drain and run under cold water. Remove the skin from the broad beans, then chop roughly with the peas. Mix both with the feta and yogurt.

6   To serve, fill the buns with the lettuce and tomatoes, followed by the mushroom patties, the broad bean salad, cress and the bun top.

SMARTPOINTS
11 per burger

"
These burgers always
go down a storm – even with
the meat eaters.
They're so tasty!
"
IMOGEN

LAVON HENDRICKS, MEMBER

Piri piri pork with roasted pepper rice

This spicy roast pork tenderloin makes a great sharing dish for a relaxed weekend lunch with friends. Serve it on a platter and let everyone help themselves.

SERVES 4

PREP TIME
20 minutes +
marinating
and resting

COOK TIME
1 hour 10
minutes

3 red chillies, deseeded and
  finely chopped
3 garlic cloves, finely sliced
1 teaspoon dried oregano
1 teaspoon dried tarragon
2 teaspoons smoked sweet paprika
2 tablespoons chopped fresh
  flat-leaf parsley
Juice of 2 lemons
1 teaspoon salt

500g pork fillet, trimmed of fat

FOR THE RICE
2 red and 2 green peppers
2 garlic cloves, unpeeled
Calorie controlled cooking spray
2 x 250g pouches microwaveable
  brown rice
Large handful fresh flat-leaf
  parsley, roughly chopped

1 Put the chillies, garlic, oregano, tarragon, paprika, parsley, lemon juice and
   salt in a food processor and pulse to form a paste. Spread all over the pork
   fillet, cover and marinate in the fridge for at least 2 hours, or overnight.

2 Preheat the oven to 200°C, fan 180°C, gas mark 6 and bring the pork to
   room temperature. Put the peppers and garlic in a roasting tin and mist
   with the cooking spray. Season and roast for 25-30 minutes, until the
   skin starts to blacken and blister. Remove from the oven and transfer to a
   heatproof bowl. Cover with cling film and set aside until the peppers are cool
   enough to handle. When cooled, peel off the skin and remove the seeds.
   Roughly chop the flesh and put in a bowl. Squeeze the garlic
   from its skin and mix through the peppers.

3 Put the pork in the roasting tin. Roast for 25-30
   minutes, until cooked through. Remove from the
   oven and set aside to rest for 10-15 minutes,
   covered with foil. Cut into 12 thick slices.

4 Meanwhile, cook the rice to pack instructions.
   Transfer to a bowl and mix with the peppers
   mixture and parsley and serve with the pork.

SMARTPOINTS
10 per serving

  See page 6

This recipe is great
— I always wanted to
learn how to make
proper piri piri.
It's so good!

LAVON

SAMANTHA IRELAND, COACH

Barbecued mackerel

Grilled whole mackerel are served with a simple side of paprika-spiced potatoes – the ideal recipe for Samantha and her family, who love going on camping holidays. It's easy to double the quantities if you're feeding a crowd.

SERVES 4

PREP TIME
10 minutes

COOK TIME
20 minutes

500g Charlotte or salad
  potatoes, cubed
1 teaspoon olive oil
1 small onion, sliced
1 teaspoon smoked paprika
400g tin chopped tomatoes

4 x 200g whole mackerel, gutted,
  or 8 x 50g fillets
Calorie controlled cooking spray
  (if cooking indoors)
Sliced cucumber and salad
  leaves, to serve

1   Bring a large pan of water to the boil, add the potatoes and simmer for 10 minutes or until just tender. Drain.

2   Heat the oil in a large frying pan, add the parboiled potatoes and onion and stir-fry for 5-7 minutes or until beginning to brown. Add the paprika, then cook for 1 minute before adding the tomatoes. Cook over a high heat for 2 minutes to heat through and reduce the liquid.

3   Meanwhile, rinse the fish, pat dry with kitchen paper and season. If using a barbecue, clip the fish into a rack or wrap it in foil. Once the coals are white, cook for about 5 minutes, turning regularly, until cooked through. Alternatively, mist a nonstick frying pan with cooking spray and cook the whole mackerel for 5-7 minutes, turning, until cooked through (the fish will just flake when poked with a knife). Fillets cook more quickly – start skin-side down until crisp, then turn and cook for a further minute, until cooked through. Serve with the potatoes, cucumber and salad leaves.

SMARTPOINTS
13 per serving

See page 6

> **"**
> I've always had fond memories of my childhood camping holidays – running around in fields, eating food cooked on the fire and feeling at one with nature.
> **"**
>
> SAMANTHA

JO WYLD, COACH

Blue cheese gnocchi bake

Guests at short notice? This easy meat-free bake is the perfect solution – with just six ingredients and only 10 minutes' prep time, it's a brilliant no-fuss dish that looks and tastes amazing.

SERVES 4

PREP TIME
10 minutes

COOK TIME
30 minutes

400g broccoli, broken into
  small florets
200g low-fat soft cheese
100ml skimmed milk

50g Stilton cheese, crumbled
500g fresh gnocchi
20g vegetarian Italian hard
  cheese, grated

1. Preheat the oven to 200°C, fan 180°C, gas mark 6. Cook the broccoli in a pan of boiling water for 4-5 minutes until just tender.

2. Meanwhile, combine the soft cheese, milk and Stilton in a mixing bowl. Season well with freshly ground black pepper.

3. Lift the broccoli from the pan with a slotted spoon, reserving the water. Cook the gnocchi to pack instructions in the same pan. Drain well.

4. Transfer the gnocchi and broccoli to an ovenproof dish. Pour over the cheese mixture and ensure everything is well coated. Scatter on the grated cheese and bake for 15-20 minutes until bubbling and golden.

SMARTPOINTS
10 per serving

“
This is beautiful – so quick and easy to make. It's a lovely creamy comfort food dish. I love it!
”

JO

JANINE LISHMAN-PEAT, COACH

Chicken, leek & cider pie

Great for dinners with family or friends, this potato-topped pie is really easy to put together. Try serving it with steamed broccoli or mange tout.

SERVES 4

PREP TIME
15 minutes

COOK TIME
1 hour

1 teaspoon olive oil
1 leek, trimmed and sliced
250g mushrooms, sliced
450g skinless chicken breast fillets, cut into chunks
400ml dry cider

1 chicken stock cube, crumbled
2 tablespoons half-fat crème fraîche
750g potatoes, thinly sliced
1 tablespoon low-fat spread, melted

1   Preheat the oven to 200°C, fan 180°C, gas mark 6. Heat the oil in a large frying pan and add the leek and mushrooms. Cook for 10 minutes over a low heat until softened. Remove from the pan and set aside.

2   Reheat the pan, add the chicken and cook for 5 minutes until browned. Return the vegetables to the pan with the cider and stock cube. Bring to the boil, cover and simmer gently for 15 minutes, or until the chicken is cooked through. Remove from the heat and stir in the crème fraîche.

3   Meanwhile, cook the potatoes in a pan of boiling water for 10 minutes until tender. Drain and set aside.

4   Spoon the chicken mixture into a 2 litre baking dish. Arrange the potato slices over the top, brush with the melted spread and season with salt and freshly ground black pepper. Bake for 25-30 minutes until golden, then serve.

SMARTPOINTS
10 per serving

✳ GF   See page 6

> **This recipe is great for the family. My husband and I have a quarter each and our son has the other half!**
>
> JANINE

JIMI APPLETON, COACH

Asian-inspired meatballs

One-pot recipes that pack a spicy punch, like these easy meatballs, are a favourite in Jimi's house – he's a fan of batch cooking and has the Tupperware to prove it!

SERVES 4

PREP TIME
10 minutes

COOK TIME
20-22 minutes

1 green pepper, quartered
1 egg white
1 teaspoon ground ginger
2 garlic cloves, crushed
4 tablespoons tamari soy sauce
500g skinless chicken breast fillets, finely chopped
Calorie controlled cooking spray

1 teaspoon natural sweetener (we used agave nectar)
2 tablespoons cider vinegar
1 bunch spring onions, trimmed and thinly sliced
225g water chestnuts, drained and sliced

1 Bring a pan of water to the boil, add the green pepper and cook for 8 minutes, then drain and roughly chop. Meanwhile, combine the egg white, ginger, garlic and 1 tablespoon of the tamari soy sauce in a medium bowl. Add the chicken and pepper and toss to coat.

2 Divide the mixture into 24 balls. Mist a large frying pan or wok with cooking spray and fry for 8-10 minutes. You may need to do this in batches. Remove from the pan and set aside.

3 Combine the remaining tamari soy sauce with the sweetener, vinegar and 125ml water. Add to the pan, boil for 3-4 minutes until thickened slightly. Add the spring onions and water chestnuts, then return the meatballs to the pan and toss to glaze. Serve with a zero SmartPoints green salad, or 120g cooked brown rice per person for an extra 4 SmartPoints per serving.

2 SmartPoints value

SMARTPOINTS
2 per serving

GF See page 6

> " I love Asian-style food. This is a tasty, aromatic recipe which is perfect for batch cooking. "
>
> JIMI

Passion fruit Bellinis

MAKES 6

PREP TIME
5 minutes

Peel and de-stone 2 ripe **peaches**. Whizz them into a purée using a stick blender and divide the purée equally between 6 Champagne flutes or saucers. Cut 3 **passion fruits** in half, scoop out the flesh and add it to the glasses. Pour over 750ml **Prosecco** (you'll have a bit left over for top-ups) and stir, then serve immediately.

V **GF*** **4** SmartPoints value

SMARTPOINTS
4 per cocktail

Ginger Pimm's

MAKES 4

PREP TIME
5 minutes +
macerating

Combine 140ml **Pimm's** and 50ml gin in a tall serving jug, stir in some sliced **strawberries** and whole raspberries and some fresh mint leaves and leave to macerate for up to an hour. Top with 500ml **diet ginger beer** and 300ml **diet lemonade** and serve over ice.

V **GF*** **3** SmartPoints value

SMARTPOINTS
3 per cocktail

> "We love these glam cocktails – they're great for special occasions."
>
> SARAH FROM THE WW KITCHEN TEAM

Drinks for entertaining

Bring a bit of fruity fizz to your next party or barbecue with the WW Kitchen Team's favourite SmartPoints friendly cocktails.

Blackberry fizz

MAKES 4

PREP TIME
5 minutes

Put 2 teaspoons **demerara sugar** and a handful of **fresh mint leaves** in a small jug and muddle using a cocktail muddler. If you don't have one, use the end of a rolling pin or the back of a spoon. Add 100g **blackberries** and crush just a little. Pour over 75ml **vodka** and stir. Half-fill 4 tumblers with ice cubes and spoon over the fruit and vodka mixture. Top with diet tonic water and serve garnished with **lime wedges** and extra mint leaves.

(V) **(GF*)** **(2 SmartPoints value)**

SMARTPOINTS 2 per cocktail

Champagne berry cocktail

MAKES 2

PREP TIME
5 minutes

Put a **blackberry**, a **raspberry** and a small handful of **blackcurrants** and **redcurrants** into 2 Champagne saucers. Add 1 teaspoon **elderflower cordial** and a few fresh mint leaves to each glass, muddle lightly with the end of a teaspoon and leave for 5 minutes or so for the flavours to mingle. Then top each glass with 125ml **Champagne**, stir and serve.

(V) **(GF*)** **(4 SmartPoints value)**

SMARTPOINTS 4 per cocktail

*See page 6

"I discovered a love for **healthy eating** after joining Weight Watchers."
◀ MELISSA

"I love eating **fresh, home-cooked** meals."
ELAINE ▶

"I try to keep **mealtimes exciting** so I never feel I'm depriving myself."
LISA ▶

Make it a fakeaway

Kebabs, curries, Chinese, pizza… takeaways are undeniably tasty, but not as healthy as they could be. Unless, of course, you create your own.

MELISSA VANZANT-BIRCH, MEMBER

Yasai yaki soba

This noodle dish is a must-try if, like Melissa, you love Japanese flavours. You can use any vegetables that you have to hand and if you're not a fan of spice, simply leave out the sriracha chilli sauce.

SERVES 2

PREP TIME
2 minutes

COOK TIME
10 minutes

2 tablespoons mirin
2 tablespoons dark soy sauce
2 tablespoons sake
2 tablespoons yellow bean or
  miso paste

1 tablespoon sriracha chilli sauce
  (optional)
120g soba noodles
Calorie controlled cooking spray
300g pack stir-fry vegetables

1   Put the mirin, soy sauce, sake, yellow bean or miso paste and sriracha sauce, if using, in a small pan and bring to the boil. Reduce the heat and simmer for 2 minutes, then set aside.

2   Meanwhile, simmer the noodles in a pan of boiling water for 5 minutes, or until just tender. Drain and set aside.

3   Mist a wok or large frying pan with cooking spray and put over a high heat. Add the vegetables and stir-fry for 3 minutes, or until the vegetables are tender. Add the noodles and sauce, and toss to mix. Stir-fry for 2 minutes, making sure everything is well-coated in the sauce. Serve immediately.

  SMARTPOINTS
11 per serving

> My step-daughter **loves** this and it takes less than **15 minutes** to make, so we eat it almost every week!
>
> MELISSA

SARAH COOK, FOOD STYLIST & MEMBER

Fish & chips

Still one of Britain's favourite meals, fish and chips can definitely be on your Friday night menu. This version with a crispy polenta coating instead of batter, is a favourite of Sarah's.

SERVES 4

PREP TIME
20 minutes

COOK TIME
40 minutes

Calorie controlled cooking spray
2 large potatoes, cut into 1cm
   wedges
1 tablespoon white or red
   wine vinegar
½ teaspoon salt
1½ teaspoons black pepper

100g dry polenta, plus
   2 tablespoons for dusting
1 egg, beaten
120ml skimmed milk
1 teaspoon lemon zest
1 teaspoon dried mixed herbs
4 x 150g cod or haddock fillets

1   Preheat the oven to 200°C, fan 180°C, gas mark 6. Mist two large baking trays with the cooking spray.

2   Put the potatoes in a large bowl and add the vinegar, salt and pepper, then toss to coat. Arrange them on one of the prepared baking trays and bake for 20 minutes.

3   Meanwhile, in a mixing bowl, combine the polenta with the beaten egg, milk, zest, herbs and a little more salt and pepper; mix well to make a thick batter. Dust the fish with the extra 2 tablespoons of polenta, dip in the batter and turn to coat both sides. Put the fish on the second prepared baking tray and spoon over any remaining batter, patting the fish to achieve an even coating.

4   Bake the fish with the chips for a further 18-20 minutes, until both are tender and the polenta batter is just starting to crack.

SMARTPOINTS
7 per serving

   See page 6

> "This is even **better** than the takeaway version! It's really **crispy** and **delicious** without being oily."
>
> SARAH

ELAINE BARNES, MEMBER

Beef satay with sweet & sour salad

This Asian-inspired beef satay dish is a huge hit with Elaine, who was looking for gluten-free meal ideas. The strips of steak are marinated in lime and honey, then griddled and served with a delicious peanut sauce.

SERVES 2

PREP TIME
20 minutes

COOK TIME
5 minutes

250g frying steak, cut into 10 strips
2 teaspoons clear honey
¼-½ red chilli, diced
Calorie controlled cooking spray
Lime wedges, to serve

FOR THE SATAY SAUCE
30g crunchy peanut butter
5g peeled fresh ginger, finely grated
1 small garlic clove, finely grated
½ teaspoon soy sauce
½ tablespoon sweet chilli sauce

¼ teaspoon Thai fish sauce
25ml coconut water

FOR THE SALAD
1 teaspoon caster sugar
2 teaspoons white wine vinegar
¼ cucumber, chopped
75g radishes, sliced
1 Little Gem lettuce, shredded
2 spring onions, sliced
Small handful fresh coriander leaves

1 Soak 10 wooden skewers in warm water. Flatten out the steak strips to make them a bit thinner (a rolling pin is ideal for this).

2 Mix all the satay sauce ingredients together. Put the beef strips in a dish and spoon ½ tablespoon satay sauce over (put the rest in a small serving bowl). Add the honey and chilli and turn to coat, then set aside until ready to cook.

3 To make the salad, dissolve the caster sugar with the vinegar in a bowl and add the cucumber and radishes. Cover and set aside.

4 Thread the beef onto the skewers. Heat a griddle pan until really hot and mist with cooking spray. Cook for 2 minutes on each side, or until charred and just cooked. You may need to do this in batches.

5 Add the remaining ingredients to the salad and serve with the beef, satay sauce and lime wedges.

SMARTPOINTS
9 per serving

See page 6

“

I adore all these **yummy** Asian flavours, so I always look forward to making this dish!

”

ELAINE

ANABEL BONNER, MEMBER

Goan prawn curry

Indian takeaways often use cream and butter. This fragrant curry uses lighter coconut milk, but still gives you loads of rich flavour.

SERVES 4

PREP TIME
15 minutes

COOK TIME
25 minutes

Calorie controlled cooking spray
1 large onion, grated
4cm-piece fresh ginger, peeled
  and grated
3 garlic cloves, chopped
1 green chilli, deseeded and
  finely chopped
2 tomatoes, deseeded and chopped
1 teaspoon ground turmeric
1 tablespoon curry powder

3 cardamom pods, split
150ml reduced-fat coconut milk
100ml fish stock, made with
  ½ a cube
100g sugar snap peas
400g raw peeled king prawns
Juice of 1 lime
½ teaspoon caster sugar
2 tablespoons chopped fresh
  coriander

1   Heat a large pan over a medium heat, mist with the cooking spray and add the onion. Cover and cook for 8 minutes, until softened.

2   Add the ginger, garlic and chilli to the pan and cook for 1 minute. Add the tomatoes, spices, coconut milk and stock. Bring to the boil, then reduce the heat and simmer, part-covered, for 8 minutes, until reduced and starting to thicken.

3   Stir in the sugar snap peas, prawns and lime juice and cook for 3-4 minutes, until the prawns are cooked through. Season to taste with salt and freshly ground black pepper, then add the sugar and half the coriander.

4   Serve the curry garnished with the remaining coriander.

SMARTPOINTS
3 per serving

GF See page 6

> " This is a great **Saturday** meal in for me and the hubby. I love **prawns** and curry, so it's perfect! "
>
> ANABEL

LISA WALMSLEY, MEMBER

Pad Thai

This delicious noodle dish is as easy to make as it is popular – everyone loves it! The fish sauce helps give it that authentic flavour and it also seasons the dish so there's no need for extra salt.

SERVES 2

PREP TIME
10 minutes

COOK TIME
5-6 minutes

2 teaspoons vegetable oil
½ red onion, finely sliced
2 garlic cloves, finely sliced
1 red chilli, deseeded and
   finely sliced
180g raw prawns
Juice of 1 lime, plus lime
   wedges to serve
1 tablespoon fish sauce

300g wok-ready ribbon
   rice noodles
125g bean sprouts
1 egg
2 spring onions, chopped
Large handful fresh coriander,
   roughly chopped
15g roasted peanuts, chopped

1   Heat the oil in a wok or large frying pan, then add the red onion, garlic and chilli and stir-fry for 1 minute. Add the prawns and cook until they start to turn pink, then add the lime juice and fish sauce and cook for another minute.

2   Add the noodles and bean sprouts to the wok and toss everything together using tongs or two forks, until the noodles separate. Make a well in the centre of the mixture and crack in the egg. Stir with a spatula until the egg is semi-cooked, then mix into the noodles with half the spring onion and coriander.

3   Divide between 2 shallow bowls and top with the peanuts and remaining spring onion and coriander. Serve with the lime wedges.

SMARTPOINTS
11 per serving

   See page 6

> **"** We often go to Thai restaurants, but I'd never been brave enough to cook Thai dishes myself until I tried this. It's so quick and easy to make. **"**
>
> LISA

VICKY NEWMAN, MEMBER

Thai-style pork with curry sauce

Stir-frying is a really quick and easy way to create healthy meals with lots of flavour, like this pork mince dish inspired by a Thai restaurant favourite.

SERVES 4

PREP TIME
15 minutes

COOK TIME
10-12 minutes

240g flat rice noodles
2 teaspoons sunflower oil
1 stick fresh lemongrass, outer
    leaves removed, finely chopped
5cm-piece fresh ginger, grated
1 red chilli, deseeded and diced
1 garlic clove, crushed
300g lean pork mince

2 carrots, cut into ribbons
2 pak choi, leaves separated
2 tablespoons soy sauce

FOR THE CURRY SAUCE
2 tablespoons Thai green curry paste
200ml reduced-fat coconut milk
Juice of 1 lime, plus wedges to serve

1   Bring a pan of water to the boil, add the noodles and cook to pack instructions. Drain and set aside.

2   Heat the oil in a wok or large frying pan, add the lemongrass, ginger, chilli and garlic and stir-fry for 1 minute. Add the mince and cook on a high heat until browned, breaking up any lumps. Stir in the carrot, pak choi and soy sauce and cook until the pak choi has wilted. Toss the noodles in the wok until combined and hot.

3   Meanwhile, prepare the sauce. Gently heat the curry paste in a small pan until sizzling, add the coconut milk and lime juice and simmer for 1-2 minutes.

4   Serve the stir-fry with the lime wedges and curry sauce on the side.

SMARTPOINTS
12 per serving

See page 6

" I love making takeaway-
style dishes for
girly weekends
with lots of friends.
"
VICKY

BECKY JONES, MEMBER

Four seasons pizza

This simple four-in-one pizza is the answer if, like Becky, everyone in your family likes different things. Keeping them all happy is not a problem as there's something on it for everyone!

SERVES 4

PREP TIME
10 minutes

COOK TIME
10 minutes

2 tablespoons tomato pasta sauce
110g Turkish-style flatbread
1 thin slice Parma ham, torn
50g tinned pineapple chunks
  in juice, drained
40g tinned tuna in water, drained
3 teaspoons sweet chilli sauce
6 slices pepperoni
½ green pepper, deseeded
  and sliced

1 tablespoon caramelised red
  onion chutney
25g soft mild goat's cheese
20g cooked skinless chicken
  breast fillet, shredded
1 tablespoon tinned sweetcorn
2 cherry tomatoes, halved
25g light mozzarella, torn
Fresh rocket leaves, to serve

1. Preheat the oven to 200°C, fan 180°C, gas mark 6. Spread 1 tablespoon of the pasta sauce over a quarter of the flatbread base. Top with the Parma ham and pineapple.

2. Mix the remaining pasta sauce with the tuna and 2 teaspoons of the sweet chilli sauce, and spread the mixture over a quarter of the base. Top with the pepperoni and green pepper.

3. Spread the onion chutney over the third quarter of the base and dot over the goat's cheese.

4. Put the chicken breast, sweetcorn and halved cherry tomatoes on the final quarter of the base. Top with the mozzarella and drizzle over the remaining sweet chilli sauce.

5. Put the pizza onto a baking sheet and cook for 8-10 minutes until crisp. Scatter over the rocket to serve.

SMARTPOINTS PER QUARTER
Ham & pineapple, 4
Tuna, 11
Goat's cheese, 10
Chicken, 5
or 8 per quarter pizza if everyone has an equal piece of each.

> I've thrown away all my takeaway menus to encourage me to cook!
>
> BECKY

KERRYN NEWMAN, MEMBER

Piri piri chicken kebabs

This healthy version of a takeaway kebab is one of Kerryn's favourite meals to cook at home. The slaw has a healthy yogurt-based dressing, which goes perfectly with the spicy grilled chicken.

SERVES 2

PREP TIME
10 minutes

COOK TIME
25 minutes

100g brown rice
250g skinless chicken breast fillet, cut into small chunks
2 teaspoons lemon juice
½ teaspoon piri piri seasoning
1 teaspoon sunflower or olive oil

FOR THE SLAW
¼ white cabbage, shredded
¼ red onion, finely sliced
1 carrot, coarsely grated
2 teaspoons lemon juice
50g low-fat natural yogurt
½ teaspoon caraway seeds (optional)
Few fresh parsley or coriander leaves

1   Cook the rice to pack instructions. Heat the grill and line the grill pan with kitchen foil. If you're using wooden skewers, soak them in warm water for a few minutes to stop them from burning.

2   Meanwhile, put the chicken in a bowl with the lemon juice, piri piri seasoning and oil and set aside. Combine the slaw ingredients, mix well and season to taste.

3   Thread the chicken onto 2 skewers and grill, turning, for around 10 minutes, or until golden and cooked through. When the rice is cooked, drain and serve with the chicken and slaw.

SMARTPOINTS
8 per serving

GF   See page 6

> " This is great as I can throw it together quickly in the evenings and it's really tasty. "
>
> KERRYN

ARUNA & SONALI DEVANI, MEMBERS

Mushroom & pepper curry

This speedy veggie curry was created by Aruna, who was inspired to make her favourite family recipes healthier after joining Weight Watchers with daughter Sonali. Without the naan, it's only 1 SmartPoint per serving.

SERVES 4

PREP TIME
5 minutes

COOK TIME
15 minutes

1 teaspoon vegetable oil
1 teaspoon mustard seeds
1 onion, finely chopped
400g button mushrooms, halved or quartered
½ green and ½ yellow pepper, each deseeded and cut into chunks
1 tablespoon ground coriander

1 teaspoon ground turmeric
1½ teaspoons ground chilli powder
2 beef tomatoes, chopped
4 tablespoons 0% fat natural Greek yogurt
4 mini naan breads, warmed, to serve

1 Heat the oil in a medium frying pan set over a high heat. Add the mustard seeds and onion and cook for 3-4 minutes, until the onion is golden and the seeds have started to pop.

2 Add the mushrooms, peppers, ground coriander, turmeric and chilli powder. Stir well, then cook for 4-5 minutes over a medium heat until the vegetables are just tender but still have a bit of crunch.

3 Stir in the tomatoes and cook for 2-3 minutes until the curry mixture has thickened slightly.

4 Divide the vegetable curry between bowls and serve each topped with 1 tablespoon of Greek yogurt, with the warmed naan bread on the side.

SMARTPOINTS
4 per serving

Tip
To make this No Count, serve with brown rice instead of the naan.

> "
> Mum's food is the
> best. Everything
> I know about food
> and cooking, I've
> learned from her;
> she's the maestro.
> "
>
> SONALI

LISA COLEMAN, MEMBER

Chicken jalfrezi

A takeaway classic, jalfrezi is made healthier with lots of vegetables added into the mix. Serve it with a dollop of Greek yogurt for a touch of creaminess.

SERVES 2

PREP TIME
5 minutes

COOK TIME
35 minutes

2 x 125g skinless chicken breast fillets
2 teaspoons garam masala
1 teaspoon ground coriander
1 red chilli, finely chopped
3 garlic cloves, crushed
2cm-piece fresh ginger, grated
1 teaspoon vegetable oil

1 onion, sliced
1 green pepper, deseeded and sliced
1 x 400g tin cherry tomatoes
100g brown rice
Handful fresh coriander, chopped
1 tablespoon 0% fat natural Greek yogurt

1 Make slashes in the chicken breasts. Mix the spices, chilli, garlic and ginger with 1 teaspoon cold water to make a paste. Rub the paste into the chicken breasts and set aside to marinate.

2 Heat the oil in a pan over a medium heat and fry the onion for 5 minutes. Add the pepper and fry for another 5 minutes. Then add the chicken and cook for a further 5 minutes, turning once. Add the tomatoes with 2 tablespoons of water. Cover and simmer on a low heat for 15 minutes. Remove the lid, turn the chicken and let the sauce reduce for 3 minutes.

3 Meanwhile, cook the rice to pack instructions. Divide between 2 plates, top with the chicken, sprinkle with the coriander and serve with the yogurt.

SMARTPOINTS
8 per serving

 GF See page 6

> 66
> I can adapt most recipes, including this delicious curry, to No Count.
> 99
> LISA

Indian sides

Just because you're not getting your curry delivered, doesn't mean you have to miss out on all the tasty sides!

Pea & potato samosas

MAKES 12

PREP TIME
15 minutes

COOK TIME
45 minutes

Bring a pan of water to the boil, add 250g diced **potato** and simmer for 10 minutes or until soft, then drain. Heat 1 tablespoon **vegetable oil** in a pan, add 1 small diced **onion**, a chopped **garlic clove** and a 2.5cm piece of fresh grated **ginger** and cook for 7-8 minutes or until soft. Stir in 1 teaspoon **garam masala** and ½ teaspoon **curry powder**. Cook for 1 minute, then turn off the heat. Stir in the cooked potatoes, 50g frozen **peas** and 2 teaspoons **lemon juice**, then season. Preheat the oven to 200°C, fan 180°C, gas mark 6. Mist a baking tray with **calorie controlled cooking spray**. Unwrap a 270g pack of fresh **filo pastry** and halve each sheet of pastry so you have 12 squares. Take a square and fold it in half to make a rectangle. Put 1 heaped tablespoon of the filling at the bottom left of the rectangle. Fold the right corner of the pastry over the filling to cover it and form a triangle. Fold the triangle up, then to the right-hand side, and keep folding until you reach the end of the strip. Put on the baking tray and repeat with the remaining pastry and filling. Brush with 15g melted **low-fat spread** and sprinkle with 1 teaspoon **sesame seeds**. Bake for 20–25 minutes or until golden.

SMARTPOINTS 3 per samosa

7-minute naans

MAKES 4

PREP TIME
10 minutes

COOK TIME
8 minutes

Sift 200g **self-raising flour** into a large bowl, season with **salt** and freshly ground **black pepper**, then add 2 teaspoons **black onion seeds**. Make a well and add 125ml **sugar-free lemonade** then mix so you have a stiff, smooth dough. Shape into 4 rounds, each about 12cm in diameter. Heat a small pan and mist with **calorie controlled cooking spray**. Add one round of dough and cook for 1 minute, until puffed up and brown. Mist the top side of the bread with cooking spray, flip it over and cook for 1 minute. Repeat with the other rounds and serve warm. The lemonade gives the naans a light, fluffy texture.

SMARTPOINTS 5 per naan

Tip
These little naans make great pizza bases, too! Just add 1 teaspoon garlic powder.

Spiced chickpea salad

SERVES 4

PREP TIME
5 minutes

COOK TIME
2 minutes

For the dressing, whisk together 1 teaspoon **black onion seeds**, 1 teaspoon **cumin seeds**, 1 teaspoon grated **fresh ginger**, 1 small crushed **garlic clove**, 1 teaspoon **olive oil** and the juice of 1 **lime** with 1 tablespoon water. Season with **salt** and freshly ground **black pepper** and set aside. Drain and rinse a 400g tin **chickpeas**, then put in a bowl with 50g young leaf **spinach**, a third of a **cucumber**, halved lengthways and finely sliced, and 1 halved and finely sliced **red onion**. Pour over the dressing and toss to coat, then serve immediately.

2
SmartPoints
value

SMARTPOINTS 2 per serving

V | **GF**   See page 6

> " These **delicious** side dishes turn a simple curry into an Indian banquet – perfect for a fakeway feast! "

LINZI FROM THE WW KITCHEN TEAM

Something sweet

Enjoying a dessert or sweet treat every now and then doesn't have to knock you off track, and these members have got the recipes to prove it...

"My sister and I run a cafe and people always tell us they're **amazed** that they can **indulge** without going off track."

◀ NOEL

"I like to save the **treats** for weekends and make something **extra special**."

IAN ▶

"Starting my cake business in 2014 gave me an **extra incentive** to tackle my weight problem."

◀ DEBBIE

EMMA GARDNER, MEMBER

Rhubarb & ginger pavlova

This easy pavlova topped with Greek yogurt and poached rhubarb is a great choice for Emma and her husband Jason, who love having friends over for dinner.

SERVES 6

PREP TIME
15 minutes

COOK TIME
1 hour 45 minutes
+ cooling

Calorie controlled cooking spray
3 egg whites
150g caster sugar
250g rhubarb, trimmed and cut
   into 2.5cm pieces

2cm piece fresh ginger, sliced
250ml ginger beer
1 teaspoon vanilla extract
1 tablespoon icing sugar
350g 0% fat natural Greek yogurt

1 Preheat the oven to 180°C, fan 160°C, gas mark 4. Mist a large baking sheet with the cooking spray and line with baking paper. Draw a 20cm diameter circle on the paper and set aside.

2 Put the egg whites in a clean, grease-free glass or ceramic mixing bowl and whisk with an electric whisk until they are opaque and form stiff peaks. Whisk in the caster sugar, 1 tablespoon at a time, until the meringue is shiny and stiff.

3 Spoon the meringue onto the baking sheet circle and swirl to make a dip in the middle. Put in the oven and reduce the temperature to 120°C, fan 100°C, gas mark ½. Bake for 1 hour 30 minutes, then turn off the oven and leave the meringue inside to cool completely.

4 Meanwhile, put the rhubarb, ginger and ginger beer in a pan over a medium-low heat. Gently simmer for 5 minutes or until the rhubarb is tender but not collapsing. Remove from the heat and set aside to cool. Chill until needed.

5 Carefully peel the baking paper from the base of the meringue and put the meringue on a serving plate. Stir the vanilla extract and icing sugar into the yogurt then spoon it over the meringue. Lift the rhubarb from the ginger beer with a slotted spoon, discarding the ginger, and spoon it over the yogurt. Reduce the remaining liquid to a syrup and drizzle it over the rhubarb and meringue. Serve the pavlova in slices within 1 hour of assembling.

SMARTPOINTS
8 per serving

See page 6

> "
> I want to serve my guests **something indulgent.** This looks impressive and is really delicious too.
> "
>
> EMMA

NICOLA UPSALL, MEMBER

Zingy lemon meringue tart

This clever take on a lemon meringue pie went down a storm when we first shared it with members. It was created by Nicola, who was one of *Weight Watchers* magazine's 'Great skinny bake-off' finalists.

SERVES 12

PREP TIME
25 minutes +
cooling

COOK TIME
40 minutes

200g ginger nut biscuits
75g apple sauce
1 lemon (skin left on)
30ml freshly squeezed lemon juice
3 egg yolks and 2 egg whites
1 tablespoon cornflour
225g caster sugar

1 Preheat the oven to 200°C, fan 180°C, gas mark 6. In a food processor, blitz the ginger nuts to fine crumbs. Add the apple sauce and pulse until the mixture starts to come together. Tip into a 36cm x 12cm loose-bottomed tart tin and press into the corners and up the sides. Bake for 10 minutes. Remove, then reduce the temperature to 180°C, fan 160°C, gas mark 4.

2 Wash the lemon, chop into small chunks and discard any seeds. Wipe your food processor clean then add the lemon. Process until the chunks have completely broken down, then add the lemon juice, egg yolks, cornflour and 125g of the sugar. Process until you have a thick, pale yellow mixture.

3 Set a small, heatproof bowl over a pan of simmering water. Pour the lemon mixture into the bowl and stir continuously for 5 minutes, until heated through. Pour into the baked biscuit case and then transfer to a baking tray.

4 Whisk the egg whites until soft peaks form. Gradually add the remaining sugar, whisking well, until you have a thick, glossy meringue. Spoon into a piping bag fitted with a star nozzle and pipe 12 rows on top of the tart.

5 Bake for 25 minutes until the meringue is golden. Remove from the oven and let cool for 3 hours before cutting into 12 slices.

V **9** SmartPoints value
SMARTPOINTS
9 per serving

> 66
> Pastry can be high in SmartPoints. Then I discovered how to create a base using **ginger nuts** and apple sauce!
> 99
> NICOLA

NOEL LARKIN, MEMBER

Rocky road

A little bit of this chocolatey, no-bake bar goes a long way, so a small slice with your morning coffee is all you need. It's become a bestseller for chef Noel and his sister Emma, who run a cafe in Bebington, Wirral.

**MAKES
16 SLICES**

PREP TIME
5 minutes +
chilling

COOK TIME
3 minutes

135g low-fat spread, plus extra
    for greasing
100g milk chocolate, chopped
100g dark chocolate, chopped
40g golden syrup
100g mini marshmallows
100g reduced-fat digestive biscuits,
    roughly crushed

1 Lightly grease an 18 x 18cm cake tin and line with baking paper. Put the low-fat spread, milk and dark chocolate and golden syrup in a microwave-safe bowl and heat in the microwave for 3 minutes, checking every 20-30 seconds to ensure it doesn't burn, until melted.

2 Stir in the marshmallows and biscuit pieces, then tip the mixture into the prepared tin, spreading evenly.

3 Chill for approximately 2 hours or until firm, then cut into 16 slices.

SMARTPOINTS
7 per slice

> " Temptation is everywhere in catering, but keeping a **food diary** and **planning** my meals helped me to lose 7st. "
>
> NOEL

STEPH WILLIAMS, WW PUBLISHING TEAM

Fruit salad with mint & lime

This medley of fresh fruit is flavoured with a zingy and refreshing combination of lime, vanilla and mint. You can use whatever fresh fruit you like.

SERVES 4

PREP TIME
10 minutes

1 vanilla pod, split and seeds scraped out
Juice of 1 lime
2 tablespoons chopped fresh mint
250g mixed berries (we used strawberries, blueberries and blackberries), larger ones halved

2 bananas, roughly chopped
2 kiwi fruit, cut into chunks
1 peach, stone removed and flesh chopped

1 In a small bowl, mix the vanilla seeds with the lime juice and chopped mint.

2 Put all the fruit in a bowl and pour over the mint dressing. Stir well, then chill in the fridge for 15 minutes to allow the flavours to develop. Spoon into glasses or little jars to serve.

 SMARTPOINTS
0 per serving

 See page 6

> " I love fresh fruit salad – this one is **so good**. It's great for breakfast, but actually tastes **special** enough to serve as a dessert as well! "

STEPH

IAN INGLES, MEMBER

Lime & chocolate cheesecake

This cheesecake is the perfect way to end a family meal, and it's also great for entertaining. It's a favourite for Ian, who loves to cook everything from scratch.

SERVES 8

PREP TIME
10 minutes +
chilling
COOK TIME
2 minutes

50g dark chocolate, grated
100g reduced-fat digestive
   biscuits, crushed
25g low-fat spread, melted
4 gelatine leaves, cut into pieces
300g low-fat soft cheese
250g fat-free quark

75ml skimmed milk
2 teaspoons vanilla extract
2 tablespoons sweetener
25g icing sugar
Zest and juice of 2 limes, plus
   extra zest, to decorate
Green food colouring (optional)

1   Line the base of an 18cm loose-bottomed cake tin with baking paper. Set aside a pinch of the grated chocolate and blitz the rest with the biscuits in a food processor to form fine crumbs. Stir in the melted spread, then spoon into the base of the prepared tin. Press down firmly, then chill.

2   Meanwhile, put the gelatine in a heatproof bowl with 4 tablespoons of water and leave to soak for 10 minutes. Set the bowl over a pan of gently simmering water (being careful it does not touch the water in the pan) and heat until the gelatine is dissolved.

3   In a large mixing bowl, beat together the remaining ingredients, including the green food colouring, if using, until smooth and combined, then pour in the gelatine mixture and stir well. Pour the mixture over the chilled base.

4   Chill for at leas 4 hours, or overnight,until set. Decorate with the reserved grated chocolate and extra lime zest, then serve.

SMARTPOINTS
7 per serving

" My family are really open to **trying new food**. They absolutely **love** this lime and chocolate cheesecake! "

IAN

DEBBIE FENTON, MEMBER

Sticky gingerbread squares

These tea-time treats use molasses instead of sugar. They were a big hit with baking mad Debbie, who started her own cake-making business, Lois's Little Cake Company, in 2014.

MAKES 16 SQUARES

PREP TIME
5 minutes + cooling

COOK TIME
35 minutes

115g low-fat spread, plus extra for greasing
225g plain flour
1 teaspoon bicarbonate of soda
1 tablespoon ground ginger
1 teaspoon ground cinnamon

200ml dark molasses
2 eggs, lightly beaten
75g stem ginger, drained and roughly chopped, plus 2 tablespoons of the syrup

1 Preheat the oven to 180°C, fan 160°C, gas mark 4. Lightly grease a 20cm x 20cm baking tin and line with baking paper.

2 Sift the flour, bicarbonate of soda, ground ginger and cinnamon together into a bowl.

3 Melt the spread in a pan over a low heat, allow it to cool slightly, then stir in the molasses and eggs.

4 Mix the molasses mixture into the dry ingredients, then stir through most of the stem ginger (reserve 1 tablespoon for decorating). Pour the mixture into the prepared tin and bake for 30 minutes, or until a skewer inserted into the centre of the cake comes out clean.

5 Meanwhile, in a pan, warm the reserved syrup with 1 teaspoon of water. Using a skewer, pierce holes over the top of the warm cake, then brush over the syrup. Decorate with the reserved stem ginger and leave to cool completely, then cut into 16 squares.

SMARTPOINTS
6 per square

> **"** This super-sticky gingerbread bake is divine! The molasses adds a rich and delicious new flavour, which I love. **"**
>
> DEBBIE

HELEN RENSHAW, WW MAGAZINE EDITOR IN CHIEF

Hot chocolate puddings

These heavenly little puds are a real treat for chocolate lovers, and also make a brilliant dinner party dessert. Serve them without the grated white chocolate topping to save 2 SmartPoints per pudding.

MAKES 4

PREP TIME
10 minutes

COOK TIME
12 minutes

Calorie controlled cooking spray
40g caster sugar
80g self-raising flour
2 heaped teaspoons cocoa powder

2 eggs, lightly beaten
4 tablespoons skimmed milk
4 teaspoons sunflower oil
40g white chocolate, grated

1 Preheat the oven to 190°C, fan 170°C, gas mark 5. Mist 4 x 100ml ramekins with the cooking spray to coat.

2 Put the sugar in a mixing bowl and sift in the flour and cocoa powder. Make a well in the centre, then beat in the eggs, milk and oil to make a smooth batter.

3 Spoon the batter between the ramekins and bake for 12 minutes, until risen and just firm. Sprinkle over the white chocolate and serve.

SMARTPOINTS
10 per pudding

> " I love these puds still **warm** from the oven – the **gooey** centre makes them feel really **indulgent**. "
>
> HELEN

Recipe index